Learning Short-take®

DEBRIEF AND FEEDBACK STRATEGIES

A trainer's toolkit for maximizing learning activities

CATHERINE MATTISKE

TPC - The Performance Company Pty Ltd
Level 20, Darling Park
Tower 2, 201 Sussex Street,
Sydney NSW 2000
Australia

ACN 077 455 273
email: tpc@tpc.net.au
Website: www.catherinemattiske.com

© TPC – The Performance Company Pty Limited
First edition published in 2006
Second edition published in 2011
Third edition published in 2022

All rights reserved. Apart from any fair dealing for the purposes of study, research or review, as permitted under Australian copyright law, no part of this publication may be reproduced by any means without the written permission of the copyright owner. Every effort has been made to obtain permission relating to information reproduced in this publication.

The information in this publication is based on the current state of commercial and industry practice, applicable legislation, general law and the general circumstances as at the date of publication. No person shall rely on any of the contents of this publication and the publisher and the author expressly exclude all liability for direct and indirect loss suffered by any person resulting in any way from the use of or reliance on this publication or any part of it. Any options and advice are offered solely in pursuance of the author's and the publisher's intention to provide information, and have not been specifically sought.

For eBook version: By payment of the required fees, you have been granted the non-exclusive, non-transferable right to access and read the text of this e-book on screen. No part of this text may be reproduced, transmitted, downloaded, decompiled, reverse engineered, or stored in or introduced into any information storage retrieval system, in any form or by any means, whether the electronic or mechanical, now known or hereinafter invented, without the express permission of the author.

A catalogue record for this book is available from the National Library of Australia

National Library of Australia
Cataloguing-in-Publication data

Mattiske, Catherine
Debrief and Feedback Strategies: A trainer's toolkit for maximizing learning activities

ISBN 978-1-921547-07-2

1. Occupational training 2. Learning I. Title

370.113

Distributed by TPC - The Performance Company - www.catherinemattiske.com
For further information contact TPC - The Performance Company, Sydney Australia on +61 (02) 9555 1953.

HELLO.

Welcome to the Learning Short-take® process!

This Learning Short-take® is a bite sized learning package that aims to improve your skills and provide you with an opportunity for personal and professional development to achieve success in your role.

This Learning Short-take® combines self study with workplace activities in a unique learning system to keep you motivated and energized. So let's get started!

Step 1:
What's inside?

- Learning Short-take®. This section contains all of the learning content and will guide you through the learning process.
- Learning Activities. You will be prompted to complete these as you read through.
- Learning Journal. This is a summary of your key learnings. Update it when prompted.
- Skill Development Action Plan. Learning is about taking action. This is your action plan where you'll plan how you will implement your learning.

Step 2:
Complete the Learning Short-take®

- Learning Short-takes® are best completed in a quiet environment that is free of distractions.
- Schedule time in your calendar to complete the Learning Short-take® and prioritize this time as an investment in your own professional development.
- Depending on the title, most participants complete the Learning Short-take® from 90 minutes to 2.5 hours.

Step 3:
Meet with your Manager/Coach

- Schedule a 30 minute meeting with your Manager or Coach.
- At this meeting share your completed Activities, Learning Journal and Skill Development Action Plan.
- Most importantly, discuss and agree on how you will implement your learning in your role.

GET VIP ACCESS TO YOUR MATERIALS

This Learning Short-take® includes an interactive activity book, associated tools and job aids, plus a bonus eBook.

1 Visit
https://www.catherinemattiske.com/books

2 Select your book

3 Click: **VIP ACCESS**

4 Enter the code: DFS2022136

WELCOME

Debrief and Feedback Strategies
A Trainer's Toolkit for Maximizing Learning Activities

Debrief and Feedback Strategies combines self-study with real workplace activities to develop skills in delivering training feedback and debriefing learning activities.

Debrief and Feedback Strategies will guide you in evaluating your current approaches to delivering feedback and activity debriefs, and in developing new and innovative approaches to maximize learning for instructor-led, eLearning and other types of training.

Participants in training value constructive feedback over tangible rewards. The effective use of providing feedback and debriefing activities is vital for transfer of learning, participant motivation and workplace application. Learning and application opportunities can be wasted when participants fail to receive relevant information about their performance. By providing you with a better understanding of useful debriefing and feedback delivery, **Debrief and Feedback Strategies** will help you capitalize on your training sessions.

Debrief and Feedback Strategies includes the **Higher-Order Question Job Aid**, provided as a free downloadable tool.

Now let's get started!

1	**Learning Short-take® >**	**Start here**
2	**Learning Journal**	**57**
3	**Skill Development Action Plan**	**63**
4	**Quick Reference**	**69**
5	**Next Steps**	**87**

"No problem can be solved from the same level of consciousness that created it."

ALBERT EINSTEIN

> "The most useful piece of learning for the uses of life is to unlearn what is untrue."
>
> ANTISTHENES

Section 1

LEARNING SHORT-TAKE®

WHAT'S IN THIS LEARNING SHORT-TAKE®

Table of Contents

How to Complete Your Learning Short-take®	5
Activity Checklist	6
Learning Objectives	7
Let's Get Started	8
Getting started - Feedback vs. Debrief	9
Part 1 - Feedback	13
Types of feedback	17
How to provide feedback	18
Top tips for handling corrective feedback	22
Handling difficult feedback situations	28
Considerations for providing feedback for virtual learning	31
Part 2 - Debrief	37
The value of debrief	39
Structuring the debrief	41
Debrief questions	42
Debriefing role plays	47
Using the power of the group	52

HOW TO COMPLETE YOUR LEARNING SHORT-TAKE®

1. **Reflect on your skills and abilities** in delivering feedback and conducting debriefs in training, and how you use this information to improve effectiveness in your role.

2. **Complete the Initial Skills Self-Assessment.**

3. Highlight specific skill areas that you believe you could develop more. Add these to the **Learning Journal.** Add to your Learning Journal as you go.

4. When you have completed this Learning Short-take® **meet with your Manager/Coach.** In this meeting, you will jointly establish a personal **Skill Development Action Plan.**

5. **Subject to your coach's final review** and assessment, you will either sign off the module, or undertake further skill development as appropriate.

"Learning is a treasure that will follow its owner everywhere."

CHINESE PROVERB

ACTIVITY CHECKLIST

During this Learning Short-take® you will be prompted to complete the following activities:

- Activity 1 -   Initial Skills Self-Assessment   10
- Activity 2 -   Feedback - Working example of confirming feedback   20
- Activity 3a - Feedback Case Studies   24
- Activity 3b - Feedback Case Studies   26
- Activity 4 -   Overcoming Difficulties   29
- Activity 5 -   Feedback Hit or Myth   34
- Activity 6 -   Designing Higher-order Questions / Activities   45
- Activity 7 -   Create a Role Play Debrief   50
- Activity 8 -   Your Training Program Analysis   54
- Learning Journal   57
- Skill Development Action Plan   63

LEARNING OBJECTIVES

Once you have completed this Learning Short-take®, you should be able to:

- Explain the value of feedback in training and workplace performance improvement

- Use appropriate techniques for delivering feedback

- Select and apply effective eLearning feedback strategies

- Design training and other types of workplace debriefs

- Explain and list debrief questioning techniques

- Create a Skill Development Action Plan

"The mind, once stretched by a new idea, never regains its original dimensions."

OLIVER WENDELL HOLMES

LET'S GET STARTED

Participants in training value constructive feedback over tangible rewards. The effective use of feedback and debriefing is vital for transfer of learning, participant motivation and workplace application. Learning and application opportunities can be wasted when participants fail to receive relevant information about their performance.

This Learning Short-take® combines self-study with workplace activities to develop skills in delivering training feedback and debriefing learning activities. It is designed primarily for trainers who work in live face-to-face or virtual training, however is also as appropriate for those developing other types of training interventions (e.g. eLearning & self study).

In this Learning Short-take® evaluate your current approaches to delivering training feedback and activity debriefs, and develop new and innovative approaches to maximize learning.

GETTING STARTED - FEEDBACK VS. DEBRIEF

Feedback defined

As a participant seeks to improve his or her performance, feedback facilitates skill development.

Feedback lets participants know if they are on track with their learning, or if they require further assistance. It also encourages and motivates participants, providing the positive reinforcement needed to maintain a safe learning environment. Feedback occurs throughout the entire training program and is communicated mainly by the trainer to the participant.

Debrief defined

A debrief is conducted by the trainer as the final step of a learning or review activity. During the debrief the trainer checks the results of the activity, provides feedback to individual participants or the entire group, fills any remaining gaps in learning and ensures that participants are confident to move on to the next session of content.

Complete Activity # 1
Initial Skills Self-Assessment

ACTIVITY 1: INITIAL SKILLS SELF-ASSESSMENT

This assessment covers the key skills in debrief and feedback.

Rate yourself on each of the techniques.
7 is competent and confident, little need for improvement
4 is average, needs improvement
1 is uncomfortable, major need for improvement

- Note specific areas of improvement related to each skill that you would like to develop. Be sure to include your *reasons* for your rating in each skill.

When conducting training programs and providing feedback to participants, I...	Rating	Reasoning
face the real issues and don't skirt around the problem	1 2 3 4 5 6 7	
understand the participants individual needs in receiving feedback	1 2 3 4 5 6 7	
maintain self control and don't become overly apologetic or justify my feedback	1 2 3 4 5 6 7	
am able to use questions to deflect to the rest of the group who often provide the sensitive feedback that the participant needs	1 2 3 4 5 6 7	
can maintain rapport with the participant and the rest of the group	1 2 3 4 5 6 7	
can provide critical feedback which resolves the problem or behavior to my satisfaction	1 2 3 4 5 6 7	
use clear language that is positive while at the same time gets the desired result	1 2 3 4 5 6 7	
know how to give feedback to participants whom I feel are difficult or challenging	1 2 3 4 5 6 7	
put the interests of the participant before my own	1 2 3 4 5 6 7	
maintain eye contact	1 2 3 4 5 6 7	
maintain a calm tone and volume in my voice or in written feedback	1 2 3 4 5 6 7	

ACTIVITY 1: CONTINUED

When conducting training programs and providing feedback to participants, I…	Rating	Reasoning
have appropriate facial expressions, body language and gestures without nervous expressions (blushing, perspiration, etc)	1 2 3 4 5 6 7	
consider that giving feedback is a strength of mine	1 2 3 4 5 6 7	

When conducting training programs and debriefing a learning or review activity, I…	Rating	Reasoning
prepare the debrief questions ahead of time and write them in a trainers guide or other documentation	1 2 3 4 5 6 7	
consider the issues that could arise as a result of the activity ahead of time	1 2 3 4 5 6 7	
allocate enough time for a solid debrief	1 2 3 4 5 6 7	
ask a mix of open and closed questions and never ask "Are there any questions?"	1 2 3 4 5 6 7	
ensure that participants are disengaged from their role in a role in activities like a role play, before moving on to discuss what they have learnt from the role play	1 2 3 4 5 6 7	
ensure that all participants have met the learning objective of the activity before moving onto the next section or finishing the program	1 2 3 4 5 6 7	
encourage participants to reflect on how they felt during the activity and discuss this openly if appropriate	1 2 3 4 5 6 7	
consider that conducting a training debrief is a strength	1 2 3 4 5 6 7	

Now update your Learning Journal (page 57)

"*You learn more quickly under the guidance of experienced teachers. You waste a lot of time going down blind alleys if you have no one to lead you.*"

W. SOMERSET MAUGHAM

FEEDBACK

PART 1

PART 1 - FEEDBACK

"Flatter me, and I may not believe you. Criticize me, and I may not like you. Ignore me, and I may not forgive you. Encourage me, and I will not forget you."

WILLIAM ARTHUR WARD

Feedback is a crucial event in training. Participants must have the opportunity to practice new skills with constructive input and support from the trainer.

Learning is an active process. This process is greatly enhanced when participants can check their learning through activities directly relevant to the learning objectives, and obtain information about their performance. Feedback lets participants know if they are on track with their learning or if they require further skill development.

Why participants need feedback

The main reasons for providing feedback are to:

- Identify and fill learning gaps
- Identify need for corrective action
- Provide reassurance/relieve anxiety
- Reinforce desired responses
- Build confidence and motivation
- Clarify expectations and priorities.

Balancing Challenge and Support

In order to grow and flourish, living things need a balance of challenge and support. Challenge provides the motivation to act. Support is the help required for successful adaptation. Effective feedback includes both of these characteristics, with the best feedback being high on challenge and high on support.

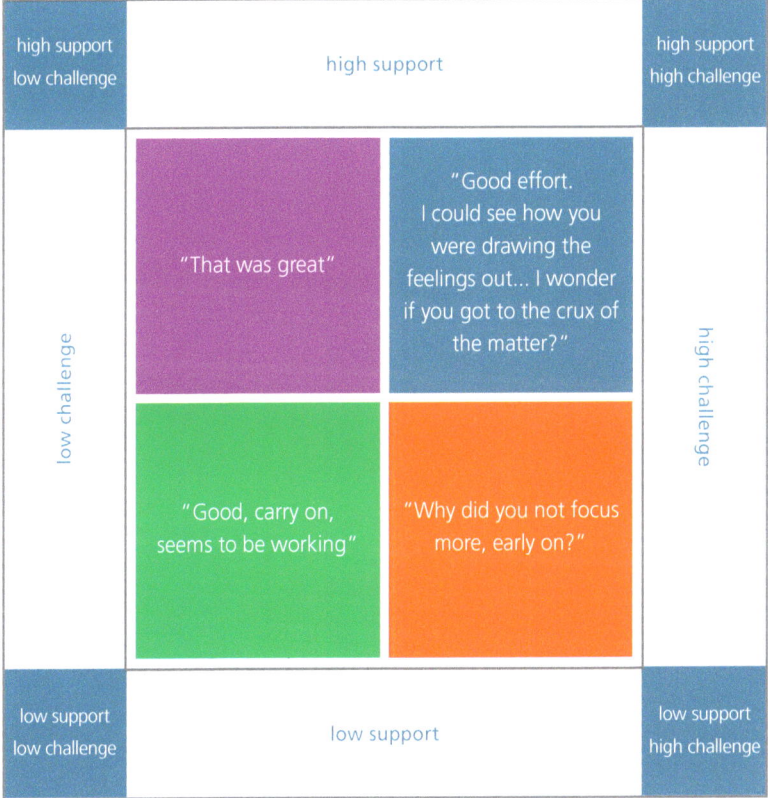

Source: *Lambeth, Southwark and Lewisham Out of Hours Project*

Feedback not Failure!

In order to maintain a safe learning environment, participants must be free to provide incomplete or incorrect responses without fear of humiliation. These responses must be handled sensitively so that participants stay confident and motivated.

The successful trainer reminds participants that it is okay to be wrong and that all learning comes with some risk of failure. Participants and trainers alike should understand that failure is only a temporary setback on the way to true success.

TYPES OF FEEDBACK

There are two types of feedback.

Confirming feedback tells the participant that they are on-track and have attained or partially attained a learning goal. This is also known as positive feedback.

Corrective feedback tells the participant they are off-track and gives them an opportunity to adapt their responses

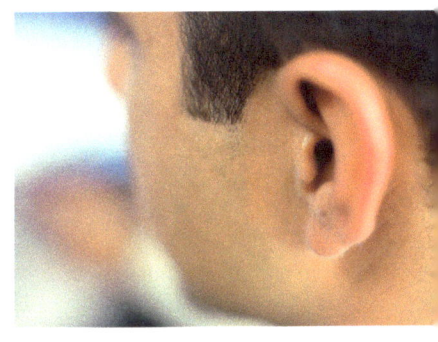

and try again. This is a sensitive task and skilled trainers are adept at providing corrective feedback in a constructive rather than critical manner, so that participants feel supported and not attacked.

Confirming vs. Corrective feedback

In order to assist the participant with their development, feedback must be present. For participants who provide a correct response the trainer has an opportunity to reassure and encourage success. Even where the response is incorrect the trainer must acknowledge the participant for their willingness to participate. The trainer then has a responsibility to clearly articulate that the response is incorrect to avoid confusion later in the program. Giving honest feedback builds participant rapport, engages participants and contributes to the eventual learning.

HOW TO PROVIDE FEEDBACK

Giving confirming feedback for correct answers or behavior

Confirming feedback should be:

Clear - Ensure that the language used by the trainer is simple and easy to understand.

Specific - State precisely what was good and why. Feedback must be detailed enough for participants to find it informative, not just flattering.

Personal - Use participants names and acknowledge them.

Giving corrective feedback for incorrect answers or behavior

Corrective feedback should be clear, specific, and personal. It also requires two additional elements:

Constructive - Suggest how the response could have been improved with detailed information and guidance. Take time to note any part of the response that was correct or appropriate.

Task Focused - Make sure it is clear the feedback relates to the task - not the participant. Feedback perceived as related to task performance will improve performance. However, feedback perceived as personal criticism may result in a decline in performance. Being specific is essential as informative feedback usually comes across as more kind and caring than a quick word of criticism. To say performance on a learning task is "poor" without providing detailed feedback is unkind and unhelpful.

Timing feedback

When is the best time to give feedback? This varies depending on context:

- For simple tasks it is best to give feedback immediately or as soon as possible
- For complex tasks a short delay may be helpful so that participants do not get "information overload"

- Although frequent feedback is generally desirable, it can be overwhelming if it is very specific, constant and detailed. For example, frequent commentary on psychomotor tasks such as swimming strokes or golf swings can overload and confuse participants.

Structuring feedback

Present your feedback in the form of a 'sandwich' - use positive, encouraging and sincere feedback as the bread to wrap around the filling of any constructive criticism so that you begin and end with positivity.

First - Tell the participant what has been done correctly by providing any confirming feedback. This will help the participant stay on track by continuing to do well what they have mastered, and make the participant feel good about themselves and the learning experience.

Then - Provide the corrective feedback that lets participants know if they were off track or responded incorrectly or inappropriately.

Finally - End on a positive note. Complete the feedback by telling the participant something encouraging but truthful. For example, "You are making good use of the case studies and really finding ways of applying this in the workplace" or "Your skills and understanding are improving steadily" or "The whole group is benefiting from your questions and analysis".

Complete Activity # 2
Feedback - Working example of confirming feedback

ACTIVITY 2: FEEDBACK - WORKING EXAMPLE OF CONFIRMING FEEDBACK

Read the following situation. Analyze the feedback used.

In a computer training session Microsoft Word Introduction, one of the participants, Sally, has completed the activity on formatting a Word document. Prior to the class, Sally had never used Microsoft Word for anything other than typing and printing a simple document.

Sally asks the trainer about the Format Painter and then uses the tool to copy the formatting in her sample document. The trainer watches closely as she uses the Format Painter tool. Sally successfully uses the tool to copy the formatting once, using a single click and then at another time, uses the tool for unlimited copies of the formatting, by clicking the tool twice.

During that interaction, the trainer says the following:

"Sally, can you remember how to use the Format Painter tool?"

[Sally responds]

"That's great Sally, you can see how all of the formatting from the first text is now applied to the second. Now try double clicking the tool."

[Sally responds]

"Well done! Now paint away. Great! Do you remember how to release the paint? Yes, that's correct, always remember to press ESC otherwise you'll be painting everything! Sally, you're doing a great job. Our next topic is long documents and you'll get plenty of practice there as well."

List the positive things that the trainer did to provide feedback to Sally.

_____

_____

_____

_____

_____

ACTIVITY 2: CONTINUED

Read the following situation. Analyze the feedback used.

In the same training session, Sally is now practicing using bullets and numbers. Sally has become a little anxious as she is having trouble moving the bullets further away from the list of text. Sally asks the trainer for assistance. During this encounter we overhear the trainer saying the following:

"Sally, what's happening, are you doing OK?"

[Sally responds]

"OK. Looks like you've started OK. Let's press undo a few times to get back to the text without any bullets applied. Now let's go slowly through the steps together. Firstly select the text. Great.

Now let's apply the bullets. Well done. OK now let's select the bulleted list again so that we can work with the ruler. Remember to select the whole list. Good.

Now, what do you notice that's happened on the ruler? That's right, but also notice that the left paragraph margin is split. Do you remember which part of that controls the first line of text in the paragraph? That's right. So we need to move the bottom section of the paragraph margin marker to the right. The key to success is to have the tip of your pointer right on it. Without clicking, just rest on it. Go slowly now. Click and drag. That's it. Well done!!

Now let's try doing that on another list in your document. You do it, while I look at what you're doing. Great. Now, can you tell me the exact steps. Fabulous! Do you feel confident now? Good.

While I'm helping Sam, why not write those steps in your participant guide and have another practice.

You're doing well Sally - remember this is all new, and it will all take time to become second nature!"

List what the trainer could have done better.

_____

_____

_____

_____

Now update your Learning Journal (page 57)

TOP TIPS FOR HANDLING CORRECTIVE FEEDBACK

1. Do not be sarcastic, critical, dismissive or disrespectful.

2. Give sincere praise and positive reinforcement where possible, without being dishonest or misleading.

3. Indicate clearly whether the response was incorrect/inappropriate/desired or not.

4. If possible, dignify an incorrect answer by indicating when it would be the desired answer.

5. Always follow-up an incorrect response - don't let misconceptions linger.

6. Correct wrong answers as briefly as possible so that misconceptions are addressed but mistakes are not dwelt on.

7. Focus on what is needed rather than what is missing, for example, "we need to also include xyz", not "you failed to include xyz".

8. Call on other participants to supply alternate responses or to build on the previous comment until the correct response has been fully elicited.

9. Hold your group accountable for providing the correct answer, and make sure it is eventually provided by either yourself or one of the group.

10. Always reinforce correct answers positively.

11. In particularly delicate situations ask participant's permission before providing feedback. A simple questions such as "is it OK if I give you some feedback?" may be all that is needed.

"After you deliver a reprimand, it's important for people to understand that you still value them as human beings."

DON SHULA & KEN BLANCHARD

Complete Activity # 3a
Feedback Case Studies

Complete Activity # 3b
Feedback Case Studies

ACTIVITY 3A: FEEDBACK CASE STUDIES

Confirming Feedback

In a time management course, Frank is asked to create a list of his long-term goals and short-term goals related to his work. Frank has always been very reactive to situations around him, and has never done a planning activity like this. He's finding the activity quite a challenge. After the break, the trainer asks the group to review their goals and share them with another participant. Frank and Martina share their goals. You are the trainer and you overhear their conversation. Martina is interested in only her own goals and is unfairly dismissive of Frank's list. Frank has created long-term goals for not only his work but also his personal life. He's broken each one of these into short-term goals with a timeframe for each. He has exceeded the standard of the set activity and gone well beyond the learning objectives. He's also very keen to know how Martina constructed her goals and is asking great questions to her.

As Frank's trainer you decide this is an opportunity for confirming feedback. Using the guidelines of confirming feedback – be clear, specific and personal, write an outline of the things that you might say to Frank about his efforts.

ACTIVITY 3A: CONTINUED

Confirming Feedback

In the same time management course, Patsy has analyzed her current workload and prioritized her activities for the upcoming week. Patsy is an administrative assistant working for four managers and continues to juggle activities. Early in the training program Patsy was very vocal about the symptoms of stress due to poor time management - it seems she has most of the symptoms!! Patsy has scheduled meetings with each of the four managers, focused time for her to be uninterrupted, and created great to-do lists. She hasn't over-scheduled herself and still has room for urgent tasks that she may be given by any of the four managers.

As Patsy's trainer you decide this is an opportunity for confirming feedback. Using the guidelines of confirming feedback - be clear, specific and personal, write an outline of the things that you might say to Patsy about her efforts.

Now update your Learning Journal (page 57)

ACTIVITY 3B: FEEDBACK CASE STUDIES

Corrective Feedback

On a systems training course, Jackie is attempting to process a sample purchase order in the new computer system. Every time she finishes the purchase order and presses 'submit' the system gives an error and beeps loudly. You are the trainer and look over to Jackie who is shaking her head and looking frustrated. What approach would you take to correct Jackie's action?

ACTIVITY 3B: CONTINUED

Corrective Feedback

You are training a course covering newly launched products. One participant, Peter, makes it known to the group early on that he knows all of the content already and doesn't need to be on the course. Peter has been with the company for eight years. In a section covering the product specifications, Peter gets the measurement and the distribution section incorrect. He has become very quiet because he clearly doesn't know the answer and doesn't want his colleagues to find out. In a whole group discussion you ask a series of questions to the group about the distribution channel for the new product. No-one answers. Another participant, Max, says aloud, "Come on Peter, you'll know - help us all out!" Peter gives the wrong answer. His answer is outdated and from two product releases ago. Max jeeringly says "No… that was from Version 2… we're up to 4 now!" Some of the other participants laugh.

As Peter's trainer, you must provide corrective feedback, however you know that Peter is now under the spotlight of the whole group. Using the guidelines of corrective feedback - be clear, specific, personal, constructive and task focused, write an outline of what you might say to Peter in response to his incorrect answer.

_____

_____

_____

_____

_____

_____

Take a break and discuss your answers with your coach or manager now, or when you discuss your Skill Development Action Plan at the completion of the program.

Now update your Learning Journal (page 57)

HANDLING DIFFICULT FEEDBACK SITUATIONS

Participant behavior	Providing effective feedback despite the behavior
No interest in the course and are dismissive of any feedback	Re-establish motivation and reward for participation ie. personal benefit of learning. Actively focus on building rapport with participants. Refocus attention by stating relevant points and refer back to activities. Re-attempt to provide feedback.
Participants who are shy or are not participating	Give strong positive reinforcement for any contribution. Make eye contact. Focus on providing 'confirming' rather than 'corrective' feedback.
Talkativeness – knowing everything, chronic whining	Build rapport by providing 'confirming feedback' and then provide very clear 'corrective' feedback. Give limited time for them to respond to the feedback while allowing them to express briefly their viewpoint and then move on. Make eye contact with another participants and move toward that person.
Sharp shooting - defend their answers or behavior in an aggressive way	Focus feedback on facts and not opinions. Ensure that facts can be quantified and move on. If unsure of the answer, redirect the question to the group or the individual who asked it.
Making personal attacks on the trainer or other participants	Disengage the attacker by firstly ignoring the behavior as any acknowledgement fuels the situation. Remain calm and positive – keep emotions in check. Recognize participant's feelings and intercept with 'confirming' feedback. Redirect issue to group or supportive individuals. If appropriate, talk to participant who was attacked privately during a break to ensure they remain engaged and maintain rapport with the trainer.

Complete Activity # 4
Overcoming Difficulties

ACTIVITY 4: OVERCOMING DIFFICULTIES

Circle or highlight which of the following feedback language and behavior is appropriate in corporate training environment.

- Make eye contact
- Allow the participant to continue being incorrect
- "You think you are very good, don't you?"
- Build rapport by providing 'confirming feedback' and then provide very clear 'corrective' feedback
- "Please leave"
- "You're hopeless"
- "Please let other people have some airtime"
- Recognize participant's feelings and intercept with 'confirming' feedback
- "Yes. You are correct. That makes a good change."
- Remain calm and positive
- "Well done!"
- Redirect the question to the group
- "Good try Paul… sorry…. but that's not correct… What about thinking about… [provide hint]… have another try…"
- "Is it OK if I give you some feedback?"
- Talk to participant privately during a break
- "You're doing very well – keep going"
- Focus feedback on facts and not opinions
- "That's a great answer"
- "Mmm… good answer… it's close to being correct… can anyone else add something to make it absolutely correct?"
- "Is it OK if I give you some feedback?"
- Discuss the benefit of learning to the participant
- Actively focus on building rapport with participants
- "That's a silly answer"
- "You're hopeless"
- Show up participant as being wrong in front of the group
- "Don't worry, I'll just talk about it with your boss."
- Give strong positive reinforcement for any contribution

Activity # 4 - Check your Answers

Check your work from the previous activity.

Appropriate	Inappropriate
<ul><li>Discuss the benefit of learning to the participant</li><li>Actively focus on building rapport with participants.</li><li>Give strong positive reinforcement for any contribution.</li><li>Make eye contact.</li><li>Build rapport by providing 'confirming feedback' and then provide very clear 'corrective' feedback.</li><li>Focus feedback on facts and not opinions.</li><li>Redirect the question to the group.</li><li>Remain calm and positive.</li><li>Recognize participant's feelings and intercept with 'confirming' feedback.</li><li>Talk to participant privately during a break.</li><li>"You're doing very well – keep going"</li><li>"Well done!"</li><li>"That's a great answer."</li><li>"Mmm…good answer…it's close to being correct…can anyone else add something to make it absolutely correct?"</li><li>"Is it OK if I give you some feedback?"</li><li>"Good try Paul…sorry….but that's not correct…What about thinking about… [provide hint]… have another try…"</li></ul>	<ul><li>Show up participant as being wrong in front of the group</li><li>Allow the participant to continue being incorrect</li><li>"That's a silly answer."</li><li>"You're hopeless"</li><li>"Please leave."</li><li>"Please let other people have some airtime."</li><li>"You think you are very good, don't you?"</li><li>"Don't worry, I'll just talk about it with your boss."</li><li>"Yes. You are correct. That makes a good change."</li></ul>

Now update your Learning Journal (page 57)

CONSIDERATIONS FOR PROVIDING FEEDBACK FOR VIRTUAL LEARNING

Modern-day learning is often conducted with the trainer in a different location to the participants, via eLearning, digital, virtual or other online methods and media. For example, a varied blend of videos, webcasts, websites, email, bite-sized learning modules and microlearning, apps, podcasts, e-books, and an endless list of digital media and platforms can be used.

These types of 'virtual learning' can be synchronous - actively linked to a trainer or other participants, or asynchronous - static and completed alone as self-paced learning, or self-study.

A key issue in adult learning is individualization and adapting the teaching to the needs of various participants. In many cases however, virtual learning programs tend to focus on converting existing face-to-face training to eLearning, digital, or other online training with little or no room to personalize. While this allows training to become more widely available, participant feedback is almost non-existent.

To make virtual learning more effective and personalized, trainers and instructional designers can use the following principles to provide participant feedback.

Feedback inclusions in virtual learning

- In order to provide feedback in an asynchronous eLearning, online or self-study environment, ensure that answers to all questions are provided. Also, ensure that suggested answers to case studies and scenarios are provided.
- Combining graphics and words boosts learning, as long as the graphics are well matched to the content. Feedback will be more effective if it includes visuals that are consistent with the text. However, graphics added just for color, interest or entertainment can hinder learning and detract from the feedback message.
- Assist participants with retention by placing associated content and activities close to each other. Display practice activities and questions close to relevant content. After participant answers display the correct answer as closely as possible (together with the original question and their answer), so participants keep in the flow of the program.
- If it is technically feasible, use audio or tools like text pop-ups to explain feedback given.
- Resist the temptation to use text, graphics or audio in an attempt to make feedback more interesting. These 'bells and whistles' added to make learning more entertaining and exciting are known as 'seductive details' and have been proven to hinder learning. Keep participants focused on your feedback by presenting it in a way that is interesting but to the point.
- Use a conversational tone to present feedback. First and second person language is more effective than formal language. For feedback to be powerful, consider adding a learning agent – a character who provides instructional advice (also known as a pedagogical agent). Research shows these characters engage participants more deeply and are especially effective for tasks like delivering feedback.

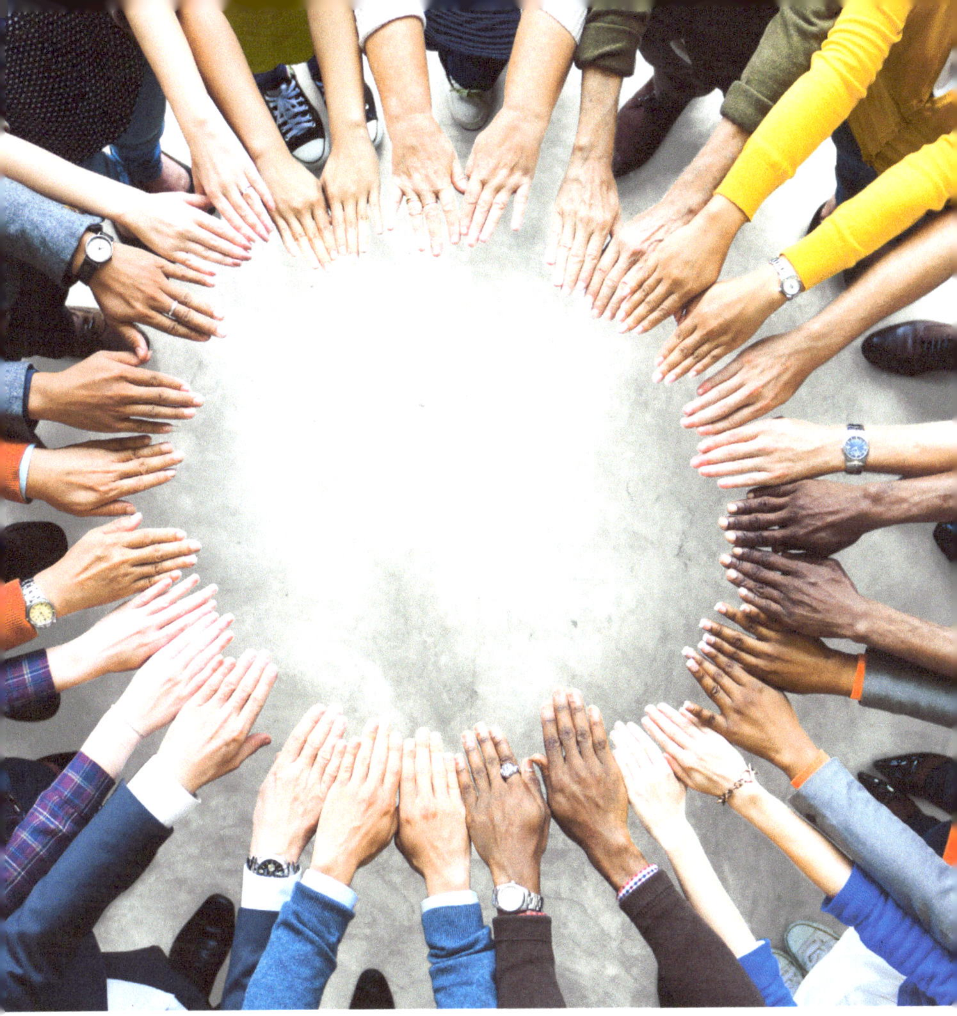

Complete Activity # 5

Feedback Hit or Myth

"Nine tenths of education is encouragement."

ANATOLE FRANCE

ACTIVITY 5: FEEDBACK HIT OR MYTH

Are the following statements about feedback true (Hit) or false (Myth)?

	Hit	Myth	If Myth, why?
1. Feedback in eLearning should be displayed on the screen separately from the question and the participants response.			
2. When delivering corrective feedback, give all the negative information to the learner first, in order to get the bad news over with.			
3. Give praise and positive reinforcement as much as possible, without being dishonest.			
4. Avoid using participants' names when giving corrective feedback.			
5. The best feedback is high on support and low on challenge.			
6. Feedback is only necessary for reinforcing desired responses.			
7. Avoid being specific when giving corrective feedback.			
8. Sometimes, feedback can be too frequent or given too soon after the event.			
9. Confirming feedback is also known as negative feedback.			

ACTIVITY 5: CONTINUED

	Hit	Myth	If Myth, why?
10. In most cases feedback should be delivered as soon after the participant offers their answer as possible.			
11. Re-establishing motivation and reward for participation ie. personal benefit of learning may help to overcome some difficulties with participants.			
12. Actively building rapport with participants allows you to develop a relationship where honest and supportive feedback is more likely to be accepted.			
13. Asking senior managers to 'pop into the course' unannounced to offer feedback to participants would be a good idea.			
14. If you try to offer constructive feedback once to a participant and they don't respond well the trainer should avoid all future attempts at either confirming or corrective feedback.			
15. In corrective feedback, to ensure the participant remembers what he or she did wrong always ask them to repeat what they did.			

Activity # 5 - Check your Answers

Check your work from the previous activity.

		Hit	Myth
1.	Feedback in eLearning should be displayed on the screen separately from the question and the participants response.		✓
2.	When delivering corrective feedback, give all the negative information to the learner first, in order to get the bad news over with.		✓
3.	Give praise and positive reinforcement as much as possible, without being dishonest.	✓	
4.	Avoid using participants' names when giving corrective feedback.		✓
5.	The best feedback is high on support and low on challenge.		✓
6.	Feedback is only necessary for reinforcing desired responses.		✓
7.	Avoid being specific when giving corrective feedback.		✓
8.	Sometimes, feedback can be too frequent or given too soon after the event.		✓
9.	Confirming feedback is also known as negative feedback.		✓
10.	In most cases feedback should be delivered as soon after the learner offers their answer as possible.	✓	
11.	Re-establishing motivation and reward for participation ie. personal benefit of learning may help to overcome some difficulties with participants.	✓	
12.	Actively building rapport with participants allows you to develop a relationship where honest and supportive feedback is accepted.	✓	
13.	Asking senior managers to 'pop into the course' unannounced to offer feedback to participants would be a good idea.		✓
14.	If you try to offer constructive feedback once to a participant and they don't respond well the trainer should avoid all future attempts at either confirming or corrective feedback.		✓
15.	In corrective feedback, to ensure the participant remembers what he or she did wrong always ask them to repeat what they did.		✓

Now update your Learning Journal (page 57)

DEBRIEF

PART 2

PART 2 - DEBRIEF

A debrief is conducted by the trainer as the final step to a learning or review activity.

During the debrief the trainer checks the results of the activity, provides feedback, fills gaps in learning and ensures that participants are confident moving on to the next session of content.

"You can tell whether a man is clever by his answers. You can tell whether a man is wise by his questions."

NAGUIB MAHFOUZ
- NOBEL PRIZE WINNER

THE VALUE OF DEBRIEF

Why is debriefing a crucial step?

Learning is evolutionary. Knowledge and learning is formed step-by-step over time. During a training session the participant should become proficient with each stage of the learning, gaining the confidence to progress to the next stage. The trainer mediates this process.

If left to themselves, only truly self-motivated participants will link the learning to real life and persist with applying their learning to their day-to-day lives. A debrief gives the participants an opportunity to talk through their learning experience and then discuss how they will transfer their learning to daily life.

If there is no debrief, there are potential issues and problems for the trainer. Here are a few problems and hidden issues that inexperienced trainers face when they make the decision (consciously or unconsciously) to leave out or avoid conducting a debrief:

- The trainer can't be sure that participants are confident about moving on.
- The trainer does not know how participants felt during the learning activity.
- The trainer devalues the training course.
- The trainer misses the opportunity to fill gaps in learning before moving on to the next topic.
- The trainer misses the opportunity to build rapport.

STRUCTURING THE DEBRIEF

As a basic strategy for debriefing, the following three-phase approach has been proven to be successful at encouraging open discussion about what happened during training. The last phase of the debrief is an important step where participants summarize their learnings and link them to real-life applications. This strategy can also be applied to debrief eLearning, digital, virtual or other types of online learning.

Phase 1: What happened?

The first phase is to check what happened. It is important that participants get to articulate this in their own words. Even if the trainer feels that their vantage point gives them a clearer understanding of what happened, this is still simply a perception, so it is imperative that participants also convey their perceptions of what happened. This phase is about returning to the experience.

Phase 2: How did you feel?

So that they can move forward to implementing their learnings, participants should express or personally reflect on their emotional state as the bridging phase between Phase 1: 'What happened?' and Phase 3: 'What did you learn?'. Phase 2 is about connecting with feelings.

Phase 3: What did you learn?

Without the vital step of linking the activity being debriefed to key learnings, trainers leave the participants at risk of wondering whether the activity had any point. A solid debrief strategy includes the trainer asking questions to elicit key learning points, fill remaining gaps and ensure that participants are ready to apply their learning. This phase is about evaluating the experience.

DEBRIEF QUESTIONS

Why are questions important?

Effective questioning is probably the single most important skill that professional trainers need in order to build two-way communication between themselves and their group. If the trainer lacks effective questioning skills the training course becomes a mere presentation, a one-way transfer of information.

Basic questions versus Higher-order questions

Sometimes, during a debrief session questions can be quite basic and closed, requiring only a yes or no or some other short factual answer. These questions are extremely straightforward, involve no depth of thought or ideas and imply nothing. If the trainer uses these basic questions they remain in the spotlight and the group is unlikely to open up. However, the power of the debrief is revealed when a trainer asks higher-order questions that call for elaborate answers, requiring examples and details appropriate to the situation.

When a trainer uses higher-order questions, the group is forced to reflect and think about its learning and is more likely to engage in a rich conversation.

Basic Question	Higher-order Question
- Does this remind you of anything? - Do you think this is a good idea? - Do you have any questions?	- How does this remind you of something you already know? - What makes this a good idea? - What questions are raised by this activity?

The value of prepared questions

The right questions are powerful tools for engaging participants, reflecting on new knowledge, and exploring how they may apply their new learning in work and life. Generally there is a strong relationship between the amount of time spent preparing appropriate questions and the effectiveness of the debrief.

Preparing questions beforehand is the surest way of knowing your questions will lead your participants to reflect on the key points. Your prepared questions should be open-ended and higher order questions that begin with what, where, which, why and how?

Thoughtfully prepared questions can help the debrief flow so well it seems to lead itself!

Returning to the experience

Questions on what happened for participants are intended to elicit their perception of the experience in their own words.

Basic Question following the debrief structure	Higher-Order Question
<ul><li>What happened?</li><li>What went well?</li><li>What went wrong?</li></ul>	<ul><li>Being as specific as possible, can you tell me what happened during the activity?</li><li>What did you do well during this activity?</li><li>If you had to do this activity again, what would you do differently next time?</li></ul>

Connecting with feelings

Questions on 'how did you feel?' assist participants in expressing their personal feeling and emotional state so they can move forward.

Basic Question following the debrief structure	Higher-Order Question
- How did you feel? - Are you confident about these new skills? - What do you think of this new idea?	- How did the [activity being debriefed] help or hinder you? - If you had to rate yourself on a confidence scale between zero and 10 (0 = zero confidence, 10 = total confidence), what score would you give yourself? Why? - What was your first thought on this new idea? What are your thoughts now?

Evaluating Experience

Questions on 'what did you learn?' are at the cornerstone of the debrief. Remember, in this phase the trainer seeks to elicit key learning points, fill remaining gaps, and ensure participants are ready to apply their learning.

Basic Question following the debrief structure	Higher-Order Question
- What didn't you learn? - What did you learn? - Do you have any questions? - Are there any gaps in your learning? - Do you think this is a good idea? - Can you use this idea? - Will you have problems using this new idea? - Are you going to use this new skill? - What will you do to reach your goal?	- What else do you want to know about this topic? - Can you summarize your learning in one sentence? - What questions are raised by this activity? - What else do you need to know before you can apply your learning? - What makes this a good idea? - What are the possibilities and probabilities of using this idea? - What are the barriers? How will you feel when you are using this idea? - So that you can put this idea into action, what is the next step? What are the remaining steps? - What milestones and critical elements need to feature in your plan for you to reach your goal?

Complete Activity # 6
Designing Higher-order Questions / Activities

ACTIVITY 6: DESIGNING HIGHER ORDER QUESTIONS / ACTIVITIES

Review the following. (Reference - Blooms Taxonomy in the Cognitive Domain)

Verbs Representing Cognitive Tasks

Lower-order / Basic	Knowledge	cite, label, name, reproduce, define, list, quote, pronounce, identify, match, recite, state
	Comprehension	alter, discover, manage, relate, change, explain, rephrase, substitute, convert, give examples, represent, summarize, depict, give main idea, restate, translate, describe, illustrate, reword, vary, interpret, paraphrase
Higher-order	Application	apply, discover, manage, relate, classify, employ, predict, show, compute, evidence, prepare, solve, demonstrate, manifest, present, utilize, direct
	Analysis	ascertain, diagnose, distinguish, outline, analyze, diagram, divide, point out, associate, differentiate, examine, reduce, conclude, discriminate, find, separate, designate, dissect, infer, determine
	Synthesis	combine, devise, originate, revise, compile, expand, plan, rewrite, compose, extend, pose, synthesize, conceive, generalize, propose, theorize, create, integrate, project, write, design, invent, rearrange, develop, modify
	Evaluation	appraise, conclude, critique, judge, assess, contrast, deduce, weigh, compare, criticize, evaluate

ACTIVITY 6: CONTINUED

Basic Question / Activity	Change each basic question or activity on the left, to a Higher-order Question / Activity. Challenge yourself to invent two or three options for each. Use Blooms Taxonomy (previous page) as a prompt.
EXAMPLE List the steps of the process	1. Demonstrate the process to two people in the class. 2. Here are the steps of three processes we've learned today. Unjumble them. 3. What is the value of steps 2 and 8 in the process.
What are the capital cities of USA, Australia, United Kingdom, Italy, South Africa and Canada?	
What is the name of this time management form?	
Identify the missing part.	
What does the term "publish" mean?	
Change one item in the following list to get the answer "3".	
Who was the author of the book "The Da Vinci Code"?	
Recite our safety motto.	
What is the Company Vision?	
Who plays the main character in the film?	

Now update your Learning Journal (page 57)

Download the Higher-Order Question Job Aid from
https://www.catherinemattiske.com/books

© 2022, TPC - The Performance Company Pty Limited. All rights reserved.

DEBRIEFING ROLE PLAYS

Why are role plays challenging?

Role playing/simulation is an extremely valuable method for learning.
It encourages thinking and creativity, lets participants develop and practice new language and behavioral skills in a relatively nonthreatening setting, and can create the motivation and involvement necessary for learning to occur.

There is little consensus on the terms used in the role playing and simulation literature. Just a few of the terms which are used, often interchangeably, are simulation, game, role-play, simulation-game, role-play simulation, and role-playing game (Crookall and Oxford, 1990). Regardless of what these activities are called the debrief is always structured in a similar way.

*"If you want to build a ship, then don't drum up men to gather wood, give orders, and divide the work.
Rather, teach them to yearn for the far and endless sea."*

ANTOINE DE SAINT-EXUPERY

Safe learning environment

When conducting a role play ensure that the safe learning environment is maintained, that all participants experience the role play and each participant meets the learning objectives.

Sometimes, role plays are conducted by just a few participants in front of the whole group. This approach is ineffective as it increases the tension for those in the spotlight and the trainer has no way of measuring if those not participating are meeting the learning objective. Instead break into groups of three and conduct a trio role play rotating the roles.

For example: in a sales training program practicing negotiation skills, the roles might be salesperson, customer and observer with each person rotating their role for specific case studies.

When debriefing a role play, the same structure of 'what happened, how did you feel, what did you learn?' is used with some variation. The role play debrief flows as follows:

1. Regroup: Firstly, before beginning the debrief ensure that all small groups have completed the role play and bring the whole training group back together. This formally ends the role play and the group advances together.

2. De-role: Asking a series of questions designed around **"what happened?"** allows participants to share their experiences and most importantly begin to de-role, that is to create a bridge between fiction and reality. Ensure that all sub-groups have an opportunity to openly share what happened. Role plays can often create emotional and challenging results. Asking **"how did you feel"** will allow participants to recount their emotions during the role play. They will most likely still talk in character. During this time the trainer simply listens and acknowledges whatever feelings are being shared.

3. Extract Learning: The trainer asks a series of questions around **"what did you learn"** with the objective of drawing parallels between the role play and real-world circumstances and events. Also the trainer seeks to draw analogies so that the group can see similarities between the workplace and the role play. The final step is to help the group apply their learning to their own specific workplace.

Complete Activity # 7
Create a Role Play Debrief

ACTIVITY 7: CREATE A ROLE PLAY DEBRIEF

Below are scenarios for three Role Plays for which you will need to write a debrief strategy. Follow the guidelines for Debriefing a Role Play in your reference manual. Write the questions in the order in which you would most likely ask them in a training situation. Try to create higher-order questions where possible.

Late No More

You have just completed the role play "late no more" as part of a management program. The situation is an employee is taking too long for lunch and is counselled by his manager. The employee has some family problems and has been spending his lunch-time with his sister supporting her through this difficult time. The manager wasn't aware of the family problems. The role play also included an observer who was asked to observe the manager and employee as the situation unfolded and was handled.

As the trainer, what questions will you ask of the manager, employee and observer once the role play has been completed?

ACTIVITY 7: CONTINUED

The Antique Car

In a sales program you have written the role play "The Antique Car" to allow participants to practice negotiating in difficult circumstances. The situation is an avid collector of antique cars is forced to sell his prize possession, one of the first Mercedes Benz's to be produced, due to personal financial hardship. The buyer quickly realizes this is a desperate sale and takes advantage of the situation. The seller is a savvy businessperson and what seems like a straightforward sale becomes a complex negotiation. The role play did not include an observer.

As the trainer, what questions will you ask of the buyer and seller once the role play has been completed?

_____

_____

Doctor, Doctor

In a communication program you have written the role play "Doctor, Doctor" to allow participants to practice questioning and listening skills. During the role play, the trainer assumes the role of a sick patient and all of the participants in the training program collectively assume the role of the one doctor. The aim is for the Doctor (all participants) to ask the Patient questions to uncover why the Patient is suffering from severe headaches. The patient only answers the Doctor's questions (which are mainly closed questions which don't reveal much information). Eventually, after a series of approximately 20 questions, the Doctors establish the reason that the Patient has severe headaches is due to a highly toxic paint that the Patient has been using to renovate their home.

You stop being the Patient and stop the role play. As the trainer, what questions will you ask the group?

_____

_____

Now update your Learning Journal (page 57)

USING THE POWER OF THE GROUP

Participants need to prove their understanding for themselves, just as much as the trainer needs to know they understand. In his book, Influence: Science and Practice, Robert Cialdini discusses the notion of social proof. If a group of people have something, or think something, then others will naturally begin to follow or at least enquire about this social shift.

Examples of this most basic social influence pattern can be seen throughout society in fashion, religion, housing trends, holiday destinations and purchasing of brand names.

Social proof can be a powerful ally in training. During a debrief session, participants talk openly about their successes with the course and the learning that is resulting. An environment of positive social proof is created in which participants listen to the views of others and work together on resolving problems and issues. They then move on to the next topic in a positive and confident state of mind.

In contrast with this, social proof can also work against the trainer. For example, if the trainer has unwittingly created an unsafe learning environment in which it is not acceptable for the participants to ask questions, then destructive social proof may occur. A few struggling participants may turn into an army of critics during coffee breaks and spread its message in the way of any disgruntled customers.

The point is, the professional trainer should ensure that participants are confident with their learning every step of the way and use social proof during a debrief to help to create a positive learning environment.

Complete Activity # 8
Your Training Program Analysis

ACTIVITY 8: YOUR TRAINING PROGRAM ANALYSIS

Choose two training programs that you or your organization currently trains or that you have been assigned to update.

For each, analyze the training program and how well the debriefing of activities is documented.

Use the suggested checklist as a guide, however, as programs may differ you may use another method to analyze the current state and possible changes.

Does the training program have the following?

	✔ or ✘
Trainers Materials (e.g. Trainers Guide, Instructor Guide)	
Clearly documented learning activities with a learning outcome or learning objective	
Clearly documented review activities with a learning outcome or learning objective	
Instructions for conducting activities that are easy for the trainer to follow	
Debrief questions for each activity	

Also, analyze the program for:
- Opportunities within the program for the **trainer** to give feedback to participants
- Opportunities within the program for **participants** to give each other feedback
- Opportunities for participants to **share their learning** with each other or the whole group
- After a major activity where a debrief has taken place, a place in the participant material for participants to **record their key learnings** (e.g. an Action Plan, Learning Journal, Learning Log etc)
- Anything else in the program that will help you to evaluate it for feedback and debrief

ACTIVITY 8: CONTINUED

Consolidating Your Analysis

Now that you have completed your analysis, what opportunities exist to make the program better in the area of feedback and debrief?

How will you go about undertaking the update?

What will be your first step?

Now update your Learning Journal (page 57)

"
"We learn more by looking for the answer to a question and not finding it than we do from learning the answer itself."

LLOYD ALEXANDER

"

Section 2
LEARNING JOURNAL

The Learning Journal is used throughout the process to record your key learnings, hot tips and things to remember.

Update your Learning Journal at anytime. Ensure you complete your Learning Journal after you finish each activity. Then turn back to the Learning Short-take® to continue your learning.

LEARNING JOURNAL

As you work through this Learning Short-take®, make detailed notes on this page of the lessons you have learned and any useful skill areas. For each lesson or refresher point think about how you could further develop this skill. Your coach will want to discuss these with you in your Skill Development Action Planning meeting.

*"…that is what learning is.
You suddenly understand something you've understood all your life, but in a new way."*
DORIS LESSING

"Act as though it were impossible to fail."
WINSTON CHURCHILL

> *"The wise do at once what the fool does later."*
> BALTASAR GRACIAN (1601-58), SPANISH JESUIT PRIEST AND AUTHOR.

Learning or Idea	Action to be taken	Result Expected

Learning Journal - continued

Learning or Idea	Action to be taken	Result Expected

"Anyone who stops learning is old, whether at twenty or eighty."
HENRY FORD

Learning or Idea	Action to be taken	Result Expected

"

"The purpose of learning is growth, and our minds, unlike our bodies, can continue growing as we continue to live."

MORTIMER ADLER

Section 3

SKILL DEVELOPMENT ACTION PLAN

Your Skill Development Action Plan is the last Step in the process. After you have completed the Learning Short-take® and all Activities, update your Learning Journal, then complete this section.

SKILL DEVELOPMENT ACTION PLAN

This is the most important part of the program - your individual Skill Development Action Plan.

You need to complete this plan before meeting with your manager or prior to on-going coaching. You will discuss it in detail with your manager or coach as he or she will ensure that you have everything you need to complete the tasks and activities.

Once you have completed your **Skill Development Action Plan** schedule a meeting time with your manager or coach to review your plan. Take your Learning Short-take® and all other documentation received during the training course to this meeting.

Remember - you have committed to your **Skill Development Action Plan**, and need to make time to complete your tasks!

"The mind, once stretched by a new idea, never regains its original dimensions."

OLIVER WENDELL HOLMES

"Whatever you can do or dream you can - begin it. Boldness has genius, power and magic."

JOHANN WOLFGANG VON GOETHE

"Imagination is the eye of the soul."
JOSEPH JOUBERT (1754-1824)

Task or activity (Be specific)	Measure (this will help you to know you have achieved it)	Date (Be specific)
Reflect on your Learning Journal. Transfer action items that you can apply to your job. Ensure that you include some 'stretch goals' and also a blend of short, medium and long term goals.	Apart from you, who else is needed to assist you in achieving your goal.	Be specific. A general date such as 'Quarter 1', 'August', or 'by end of year' is vague and more likely to result in not achieving your target. Be specific – e.g. 22nd November.

IDEAS FOR DISCUSSION WITH MY MANAGER

Ideas

CONGRATULATIONS!

You've now completed this Learning Short-take®.

Meet with your Manager/Coach to discuss your
Skill Development Action Plan.

Suggested Reading

Train for results: Maximize the impact of training through review. Catherine Mattiske

Reflection: Turning Experience into Learning. Boud D., Keough, R, Walker, D.

Appreciative Inquiry in Organizational Life. David L. Cooperrider & Suresh Srivastva

Chapter 23: Six Phases for Debriefing Experiential Exercises, by Harold D. Stolovitch and Erica J. Keeps, in ASTD Training & Performance Sourcebook, edited by Mel Silberman.

QUICK REFERENCE

This Quick Reference provides you with a summary of key concepts, models and reference material from Learning Short-takes®. We have also included some quotations to ponder.

Use this section as a quick reference to keep your learning active.

Quick Reference

> **No problem can be solved from the same level of consciousness that created it.**
>
> Albert Einstein

Feedback

As participants seek to improve their performance, feedback lets them know if they are on track with their learning or if they require further skill development and assistance. Feedback is essential for:

- Identifying and filling learning gaps
- Identifying the need for corrective action
- Providing reassurance and relieving anxiety
- Building confidence and motivation
- Reinforcing desired outcomes
- Clarifying expectations and priorities

Quick Reference

> **Learning is a treasure that will follow its owner everywhere.**
>
> Chinese Proverb

Balancing Challenge and Support

Source: *Lambeth, Southwark and Lewisham Out of Hours Project*

Quick Reference

> **The mind once stretched by a new idea, never regains its original dimensions.**
>
> Oliver Wendell Holmes

Types of Feedback

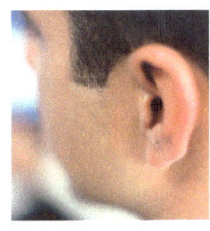

Confirming feedback:

tells the participant that they are on-track and have attained or partially attained a learning goal.

Corrective feedback:

tells the participant that they are off-track and gives them an opportunity to adapt their responses and try again. This should be provided in a constructive rather than critical manner so that participants feel supported.

Quick Reference

> **Flatter me,
> and I may not believe you.**
>
> **Criticize me,
> and I may not like you.**
>
> **Ignore me,
> and I may not forgive you.**
>
> **Encourage me,
> and I will not forget you.**
>
> William Arthur Ward

How to Provide Feedback

Confirming feedback should be:
- Clear - simple language
- Specific - Informative not just flattering
- Personal - Acknowledge and use names

Corrective Feedback should be:
- Constructive - Suggest how the response could be improved and guide. Note any part of the response that was correct.
- Task Focused - Task not participant

Quick Reference

> **After you deliver a reprimand, it's important for people to understand that you still value them as human beings.**
>
> Don Shula & Ken Blanchard

Handling Difficult Feedback Situations

Participant behavior	Providing effective feedback despite the behavior
No interest in the course and are dismissive of any feedback	Re-establish motivation and reward for participation ie. personal benefit of learning. Actively focus on building rapport with participants. Refocus attention by stating relevant points and refer back to activities. Re-attempt to provide feedback.
Participants who are shy or are not participating	Give strong positive reinforcement for any contribution. Make eye contact. Focus on providing 'confirming' rather than 'corrective' feedback.
Talkativeness - knowing everything, chronic whining	Build rapport by providing 'confirming feedback' and then provide very clear 'corrective' feedback. Give limited time for them to respond to the feedback while allowing them to express briefly their viewpoint and then move on. Make eye contact with another participants and move toward that person.
Sharp shooting - defend their answers or behavior in an aggressive way	Focus feedback on facts and not opinions. Ensure that facts can be quantified and move on. If unsure of the answer, redirect the question to the group or the individual who asked it.
Making personal attacks on the trainer or other participants	Disengage the attacker by firstly ignoring the behavior as any acknowledgement fuels the situation. Remain calm and positive – keep emotions in check. Recognize participant's feelings and intercept with 'confirming' feedback. Redirect issue to group or supportive individuals. If appropriate, talk to participant who was attacked privately during a break to ensure they remain engaged and maintain rapport with the trainer.

Quick Reference

> **Nine tenths of education is encouragement.**
>
> Anatole France

Debrief

A debrief is conducted by the trainer as the final step to a learning or review activity. During the debrief the trainer checks the results of the activity, provides feedback, fills gaps in learning and ensures that participants are confident to move on to the next session.

Quick Reference

Structuring the Debrief

Phase 1 - What Happened?
Participants return to the experience and convey their perceptions of what happened.

Phase 2 - How did you feel?
Connecting with feelings. Participants should express or personally reflect on their emotional state.

Phase 3 - What did you learn?
Elicits key learning points and gives meaning to the learning activity.

Questioning

Basic Question	Higher-Order Question
- Does this remind you of anything? - Do you think this is a good idea? - Do you have any questions? - What happened? - What went well? - What went wrong? - How did you feel? - Are you confident about these new skills? - What do you think of this new idea? - What didn't you learn? - What did you learn? - Do you have any questions? - Are there any gaps in your learning? - Do you think this is a good idea? - Can you use this idea? - Will you have problems using this new idea? - Are you going to use this new skill? - What will you do to reach your goal?	- How does this remind you of something you already know? - What makes this a good idea? - What questions are raised by this activity? - Being as specific as possible, can you tell me what happened during the activity? - What did you do well during this activity? - If you had to do this activity again, what would you do differently next time? - How did the [activity being debriefed] help or hinder you? - If you had to rate yourself on a confidence scale between zero and 10 (0 = zero confidence, 10 = total confidence), what score would you give yourself? Why? - What was your first thought on this new idea? What are your thoughts now? - What else do you want to know about this topic? - Can you summarize your learning in one sentence? - What questions are raised by this activity? - What else do you need to know before you can apply your learning? - What makes this a good idea? - What are the possibilities and probabilities of using this idea? - What are the barriers? How will you feel when you are using this idea?

Quick Reference

Debriefing Role Plays

- Regroup - Formally ends the role play and the group advances together.

- De-role - Share what happened. Create a bridge between fiction and reality.

- Extract Learning - Ask questions to draw parallels between the role play and real-world circumstances and events. Help the group apply learning to the workplace.

> **You can tell whether a man is clever by his answers. You can tell whether a man is wise by his questions.**

Naguib Mahfouz
– Nobel Prize Winner

*"If the past cannot teach the present
and the father cannot teach the son,
then history need not have bothered
to go on, and the world has wasted a great deal of time."*

RUSSELL HOBAN

NEXT STEPS

Congratulations! You have now completed this Learning Short-take® title. The entire list of Learning Short-takes® can be found on the catherinemattiske.com website.

In this section we have suggested Learning Short-take® titles for you that will build your learning. You may order these Learning Short-takes® online at https://www.catherinemattiske.com/books or from your bookstores.

Listen and Be Listened To
Transform communication in a world of distraction

Learning Short-take® Outline

Listen and Be Listened To combines self-study with realistic workplace activities to provide you with the key skills and techniques of effective and enhanced listening. You will learn to build more effective work relationships with your co-workers and leaders by tuning into key communication messages and responding appropriately. You will learn tips, tricks and techniques to boost active listening capability and discover that effective listening helps command respect from both the speakers and listeners point of view.

Our unique view of the world and personal style - based on our values, beliefs, attitudes and behaviors - affects how we act, perceive information, and communicate with others. It also influences the way we listen and how others listen to us. When we expect to hear certain things, we may pay attention to only what interests us. Our perception about a person, situation or subject influences our reception of information, and how much attention we choose to pay. **Listen and Be Listened To** breaks down the art and skill of active listening which is critical to building and maintaining effective working relationships.

Listen and Be Listened To includes an impactful **'Listening Tips' Wall Chart**, provided to you as a free download.

Learning Objectives

- Define listening.
- Explain why listening is important.
- Identify the barriers to effective listening.
- Identify their listening style and the listening style of others.
- Demonstrate techniques for active listening.
- Create a Skill Development Action Plan.

Course Content

- Part 1: Listening & Communication
- Part 2: Listening versus Hearing
- Part 3: Barriers to Effective Listening
- Part 4: Your Natural Listening Style
- Part 5: Passive Listening
- Part 6: Active Listening
- Part 7: Better Questions, Better Answers

Confident Facilitation Skills
Tools and Techniques for the Professional Facilitator

Learning Short-take® Outline

Confident Facilitation Skills combines self-study with realistic workplace activities to provide you with the key skills and techniques to become a more effective facilitator. You will be guided through a comprehensive approach to prepare for a facilitation session, focus the group, draw out ideas, manage difficult behavior, build consensus, maintain high energy, close the session, and construct customized agendas. **Confident Facilitation Skills** also includes a comprehensive reference guide of proven group facilitation techniques.

Facilitation is fast becoming a key skill for anyone who is in a team, leading a project team, heading up a working group, or managing a department. Facilitation is the skill and art of guiding others to solve problems to achieve objectives without personally giving advice or offering solutions. A facilitator provides the structure and process - enabling groups to function effectively and make high-quality decisions.

Confident Facilitation Skills includes the **Confident Facilitation Initial Meeting Tool**, provided to you as a free download.

Learning Objectives

- Define the role of a facilitator.
- Identify the key facilitation principles.
- Describe best practices related to each facilitation principle.
- Be able to differentiate between process and content facilitation.
- Identify the core practices and skills required for effective facilitation.
- Explain how to stimulate group participation and positively handle conflict.
- Create a Skill Development Action Plan.

Course Content

- Part 1: Facilitation Defined
- Part 2: The Role of the Facilitator
- Part 3: Key Principles of Facilitation
- Part 4: Content versus Process
- Part 5: Encouraging Group Participation
- Part 6: Managing Group Conflict

Adult Learning Principles 1
Understanding the Ways Adults Learn

Learning Short-take® Outline

Adult Learning Principles 1 combines self-study with realistic workplace activities for trainers, educators, facilitators and managers to develop skills and knowledge in the principles of adult learning. It will add adult learning techniques to your 'grab bag' of learning design tools for improved learning outcomes. After evaluation of your current approach to learning design, you will learn to develop new and innovative strategies to engage learners at every level. Significantly increasing participant retention and training results **Adult Learning Principles 1** will fuel your confidence in designing successful training workshops and eLearning every time.

The principles of adult learning work on the basis that we all learn differently, and the way we like to receive and interpret information varies from person to person. Trainers and facilitators who use a combination of adult learning principles to provide balance in their programs increase the chances of keeping all participants focused and engaged throughout the learning process. **Adult Learning Principles 1** will assist you in building a good mix of adult learning styles which is critical in ensuring learning, thorough participant retention and workplace application.

Adult Learning Principles 1 includes the job aid Strategies for Meeting Global and Specific Needs, the **Adult Learning Principles Quick Reference Wall Chart** and the **Activity Booklet**, provided as free downloadable tools.

Learning Objectives

- Successfully match adult learning terms with definitions.
- Determine your personal Learning Style preference.
- List and give working examples of three Adult Learning Principles – Global vs Specific, Learning Styles and Learning Types.
- Develop strategies and ideas to link Adult Learning Principles with Instructional Design.

Course Content

- Part 1: Understanding Adult Learners
- Part 2: Adult Learning Principle 1 - Global vs Specific Learners
- Part 3: Adult Learning Principle 2 - Learning Style - Modalities
- Part 4: Adult Learning Principle 3 - Learning Types - The 4Mat System

www.catherinemattiske.com